I am retired to Monticello, where, in the bosom of my family, and surrounded by my books, I enjoy a repose to which I have been long a stranger. My mornings are devoted to correspondence. From breakfast to dinner, I am in my shops, my garden, or on horseback among my farms; from dinner to dark, I give to society and recreation with my neighbors and friends; and from candle light to early bedtime, I read. My health is perfect; and my strength considerably reinforced by the activity of the course I pursue; perhaps it is as great as usually falls to the lot of near sixty-seven years of age. I talk of ploughs and harrows, of seeding and harvesting, with my neighbors, and of politics, too, if they choose, with as little reserve as the rest of my fellow citizens, and feel, at length, the blessing of being free to say and do what I please, without being responsible for it to any mortal.

Th: Jefferson

LIBRARY OF CONGRESS CATALOGUE NUMBER: 83-070669
HARDCOVER ISBN: 0-934738-04-1
PHOTOGRAPHS ©1983 COPYRIGHT 1983 IN U.S.A. BY ROBERT LLEWELLYN.
PHOTOGRAPHS © UNDER UCC 1983 BY ROBERT LLEWELLYN. ALL RIGHTS RESERVED.
THIS BOOK, OR PORTIONS THEREOF, MAY NOT BE REPRODUCED IN ANY FORM
WITHOUT PERMISSION OF THE PUBLISHERS, THOMASSON-GRANT, INC.
PHOTOGRAPHY MAY NOT BE REPRODUCED IN ANY FORM WITHOUT PERMISSION
OF ROBERT LLEWELLYN.
FOREWORD EXCERPTED FROM VOLUMES I (*JEFFERSON THE VIRGINIAN*),
III (*JEFFERSON AND THE ORDEAL OF LIBERTY*), AND VI (*THE SAGE OF
MONTICELLO*) OF THE SERIES, *JEFFERSON AND HIS TIME,* BY DUMAS
MALONE. COPYRIGHT 1948, ©1962, 1976, 1977, 1981 BY DUMAS
MALONE. REPRINTED BY PERMISSION OF LITTLE, BROWN AND COMPANY.
PRINTED AND BOUND IN THE UNITED STATES OF AMERICA BY PROGRESS PRINTING CO., INC.
PUBLISHED IN 1983 BY THOMASSON-GRANT, INC., 2250-6 OLD IVY ROAD,
CHARLOTTESVILLE, VIRGINIA 22901. 804/977-1780.

THOMASSON-GRANT

THOMAS JEFFERSON'S
MONTICELLO

FOREWORD BY DUMAS MALONE
PHOTOGRAPHY BY ROBERT LLEWELLYN

Commentary by Charles Granquist

In 1981 scholar Dumas Malone completed The Sage of Monticello, *the final volume of his Pulitzer Prize-winning biography on Thomas Jefferson,* Jefferson and His Time. *"It has been my great privilege as a biographer to be intimately associated with this extraordinary man for many years," wrote Mr. Malone. "At the end of my long journey with him I leave him with regret and salute him with profound respect." The following excerpts on the significance of the building of Monticello, domestic life on the mountaintop during Jefferson's lifetime, and the character of Jefferson as neighbor, farmer, builder, and family man are taken from Mr. Malone's monumental, six-volume work.*

…THE BUILDING OF THE MANSION at Monticello in its historic form proved to be little short of a lifetime's work. Nothing else that he [Thomas Jefferson] ever did was more characteristic of him as a person and a mind. In spirit he was pre-eminently constructive, and he could not think of himself or of his house or of human society as finished. But he was not merely creating an architectural or intellectual monument; he was a deeply domestic being, making a home. Throughout his maturity his spirit ceaselessly roamed the universe, searching out the good things in it, but his heart was on his mountaintop, and if his ghost now walks it is surely there. * * *

It is best to think of his building activities in terms of self-expression. Few men in history, and even fewer who were eminent in public life, ever found more outlets for superabundant intellectual energy, but perhaps the most gratifying that he ever found as a private man was in architecture, where beauty and utility join hands. In building and perfecting his own dwelling place he found self-expression in its most satisfying form. * * *

His choice [of a building site]…revealed a sensitiveness to natural beauty which he did not often express in words. His eye, like his mind, sought an extended view. From this spot he could see to the eastward an expanse of forested country, rolling like the sea; and to the westward he could look across the treetops to a mountain wall of lavender and blue. * * *

Liberty was never anarchy to him, but freedom to seek the truth. It seemed proper enough that there should be rules in architecture as there were laws in nature, and rules were exceedingly useful to a young gentleman amateur on the edge of civilization who wanted to build a house. If that structure had not been harmonious within itself, restrained, and symmetrically proportioned it would not have been a fitting habitation for him or at least for the sort of man he aspired to be. What he valued most in classical antiquity he prized in architecture: simplicity, serenity, and reserve—coupled with the sort of dignity which seemed appropriate to his majestic site. * * *

The mansion house that Jefferson had been building and rebuilding for some forty years…was essentially finished, along with its dependencies [by 1809]. Writing Benjamin H. Latrobe, the American whose architectural judgment he most valued and probably most feared, Jefferson observed: "My essay in Architecture has been so much subordinated to the law of convenience, and affected also by the circumstances of change in the original design, that it is liable to some unfavorable and just criticisms. But what nature has done for us is sublime and beautiful and unique." Visitors to Monticello in the early years of his retirement had much to say about nature, especially in connection with the approach to the house—up an "abrupt mountain" or a "steep savage hill," through "ancient forest-trees." Jefferson himself said that his grounds were still largely in their majestic native woods with close undergrowth. On the ascent nature appeared untamed, and viewed from the summit, five hundred feet above the Rivanna River, the vast panorama of forest and mountain was still little marred by the hand of man. Looking at the "spacious and splendid structure" that crowned the height, one observer said: "Here, in this wild and sequestered retirement, the eye dwells with delight on the triumph of art over nature, rendered the more impressive by the unreclaimed condition of all around."

It would be nearer the truth to say that nature and art appeared here in notable conjunction, reflecting the deep feeling of Jefferson for them both. Also, his architectural creation represented a distinctive blend of the functional with the aesthetic. The connection of the service wings to the main house by covered passageways provided an excellent example of his practicality; and he manifested his modernity by filling his mansion with convenient devices and flooding it with light. Yet his orders—Doric, Ionic,

Corinthian, and Attic—were designed in strict accordance with those of Palladio, while the friezes in the various rooms were adapted from the entablatures of Roman temples. His entrance hall and parlor were filled with busts and paintings. (There were too many paintings, in fact, and the entrance hall was so filled with specimens of natural history that it was already referred to as a museum.) He had provided for himself a habitation befitting his extraordinarily diverse and well-rounded personality. It was an expression of his love of privacy, his elevation of spirit, his sophisticated taste, his utilitarianism, his desire for self-sufficiency. * * *

Considering his times, he went far toward attaining *confort moderne*. In another respect this inveterate classicist showed himself to be very modern in spirit; by the use of long windows and French doors, besides supplementary skylights in the dining room and his own quarters, he suffused the first floor of his gracious house with brightness. It was a fitting habitation for a lavish dispenser of hospitality who sought for himself both spaciousness and privacy and who believed that light and liberty go together. * * *

Few things that Jefferson ever did manifested so impressively his unquenchable optimism and his infinite capacity for taking pains.... * * *

At the beginning of his retirement at Monticello he established a regimen from which he departed little thereafter. He continued to rise by daybreak—that is, as soon as he could make out the hands of a clock he kept beside his bed. He then recorded the temperature. Sometimes his overseer observed him walking on the terrace in the dawn's early light. Usually he started on his necessary correspondence as soon as he could, hoping to get this done by breakfast. Judging from the accounts of visitors, that meal was at nine. One wonders if he had tea or coffee when he arose. At first he seems to have managed to visit his garden and shops and begin to ride about his place soon after breakfast. This he did for health and pleasure, and also to note the state of his property and crops. When his correspondence increased, with the passing months, he had to stay indoors longer, but even then he generally began his daily ride by noon. On this he customarily wore a pair of overalls. By all accounts he was an uncommonly fine horseman, and in extreme old age he said that life would have been unbearable without this daily revival. His ride lasted until he came in for dinner, a meal that seems to have generally begun about four in the afternoon and to have continued long. He said that he gave the time from dinner to dark to the society of neighbors and friends, and that from candlelight to early bedtime he read. When there were no special guests he may have done this in the company of members of his family, who were engaged in sewing or knitting or something else. According to some accounts, however, he customarily retired to his quarters after tea, which was served about seven. * * *

His daughter Martha, with her large and growing brood, lived with him at Monticello. ...He had a dozen grandchildren altogether, including Francis Eppes, the son of his deceased daughter Maria. They adored and revered the kindly patriarch and contributed greatly to his happiness. His hospitality was imposed upon by relatives, but he bore with equanimity his responsibilities as the head of the clan. The physician who attended him in his last months said that no one could have been more amiable in domestic relations. Life at Monticello was not always tranquil, but Jefferson was at his best as a family man. * * *

Though he was not the sort of man to speak above a whisper about anything so sacred, memories of his ever-lamented wife were sure to linger at Monticello.... Yet there never was any doubt...that this was *his* house in the fullest sense. He planned it in its successive phases, he directed its construction, he selected its furnishings, through the years he developed the design of its grounds. It was his home, his body, the center of his personal universe. Also, on this entrancing spot he erected what was to prove an enduring monument. He was painfully long in doing it, and at the end he was aware that it was not beyond just criticism on purely architectural grounds, as indeed it was not on grounds of mere utility; but as the reflection of the mind, the taste, the individuality of a great man Monticello remains unique.

Dumas Malone

RISING WITH THE SUN

WHEN I CROSSED THE RIVANNA, a wild and romantic little river, which flows at the foot of the mountain, my heart beat,—I thought I had entered, as it were, the threshold of his dwelling, and I looked around everywhere expecting to meet with some trace of his super-intending care. In this I was disappointed, for no vestige of the labor of man appeared; nature seemed to hold an undisturbed dominion. We began to ascend this mountain, still as we rose I cast my eyes around, but could discern nothing but untamed woodland, after a mile's winding upwards, we saw a field of corn, but the road was still wild and uncultivated. I every moment expected to reach the summit, and felt as if it was an endless road; my impatience lengthened it, for it is not two miles from the outer gate on the river to the house. At last we reached the summit, and I shall never forget the emotion the first view of this sublime scenery excited.

—MARGARET BAYARD SMITH

All men who have attended to the workings of the human mind, who have seen the false colors under which passion sometimes dresses the actions and motives of others, have seen also those passions subsiding with time and reflection, dissipating like mists before the rising sun, and restoring to us the sight of all things in their true shape and colors.

MR. JEFFERSON WAS ALWAYS AN EARLY RISER—arose at daybreak or before. The sun never found him in bed. I used sometimes to think, when I went up there *very* early in the morning, that I would find him in bed; but there he would be before me, walking on the terrace.

—EDMUND BACON

*A*ll my wishes end, where I hope my days will end, at Monticello. Too many scenes of happiness mingle themselves with all the recollections of my native woods and fields, to suffer them to be supplanted in my affection by any other.

It is neither wealth nor splendor, but tranquillity and occupation, which give happiness.

THE FINE ART OF SHELTER

WE MAY SAFELY AVER, that Mr. Jefferson is the first American who has consulted the fine arts to know how he should shelter himself from the weather.

—MARQUIS DE CHASTELLUX

AT HOME, he desired to live like his neighbors, in the plain hospitality of a Virginia gentleman.

—THOMAS JEFFERSON RANDOLPH

A rchitecture is my delight, and putting up and pulling down, one of my favorite amusements.

THE HOUSE SERVANTS were Betty Brown, Sally, Critta, and Betty Hemings, Nance, and Ursula. ...They have often told my wife that when Mrs. Jefferson died they stood around the bed. Mr. Jefferson sat by her, and she gave him directions about a good many things that she wanted done. When she came to the children, she wept and could not speak for some time. Finally... she told him she could not die happy if she thought her...children were ever to have a step-mother brought in over them. Mr. Jefferson promised her solemnly that he would never marry again. And he never did. He was then quite a young man and very handsome, and I suppose he could have married well; but he always kept that promise.

—EDMUND BACON

He who receives an idea from me, receives instruction himself without lessening mine; as he who lights his taper at mine, receives light without darkening me. That ideas should freely spread from one to another over the globe, for the moral and mutual instruction of man, and improvement of his condition, seems to have been peculiarly and benevolently designed by nature, when she made them, like fire, expansible over all space, without lessening their density in any point, and like the air in which we breathe, move, and have our physical being, incapable of confinement or exclusive appropriation.

43

The motion of my blood no longer keeps time with the tumult of the world. It leads me to seek for happiness in the lap and love of my family, in the society of my neighbors and my books, in the wholesome occupations of my farm and my affairs, in an interest or affection in every bud that opens, in every breath that blows around me, in an entire freedom of rest, of motion, of thought, owing account to myself alone of my hours and actions.

EVERY DAY, just as regularly as the day came, unless the weather was very bad, he would have his horse brought out and take his ride. The boy who took care of his horse knew what time he started, and would bring him out for him, and hitch him in his place. He generally started about nine o'clock. He was an uncommonly fine rider—sat easily upon his horse and always had him in the most perfect control.

—EDMUND BACON

*B*otany I rank with the most valuable sciences, whether we consider its subjects as furnishing the principal subsistence of life to man and beast, delicious varieties for our tables, refreshments from our orchards, the adornments of our flower borders, shade and perfume of our groves, materials for our buildings, or medicaments for our bodies.

It is a singular anxiety which some people have that we should all think alike. Would the world be more beautiful were all our faces alike? Were our tempers, our talents, our tastes, our forms, our wishes, aversions, and pursuits cast exactly in the same mould? If no varieties existed in the animal, vegetable, or mineral creation, but all were strictly uniform, catholic, and orthodox, what a world of physical and moral monotony would it be!

58

THE CHILDREN RAN TO HIM and immediately proposed a race; we seated ourselves on the steps of the Portico, and he after placing the children according to their size one before the other, gave the word for starting and away they flew; the course round this back lawn was a quarter of a mile, the little girls were much tired by the time they returned...and came panting and

out of breath to throw themselves into their grandfather's arms, which were opened to receive them; he pressed them to his bosom and rewarded them with a kiss; he was sitting on the grass and they sat down by him, until they were rested....

—MARGARET BAYARD SMITH

I HAVE RODE OVER THE PLANTATION, I reckon, a thousand times with Mr. Jefferson, and when he was not talking he was nearly always humming some tune, or singing in a low tone to himself.

—EDMUND BACON

AS A GIRL, I would join him in his walks on the terrace, sit with him over the fire during the winter twilight, or by the open windows in summer. ...I loved him and honored him above all earthly beings.

—ELLEN WAYLES COOLIDGE

*T*he greatest service which can be rendered any country is to add a useful plant to its culture.

The soil is the gift of God to the living.

That every man shall be made virtuous, by any process whatever, is, indeed, no more to be expected, than that every tree shall be made to bear fruit, and every plant nourishment. The brier and bramble can never become the vine and olive; but their asperities may be softened by culture, and their properties improved to the usefulness in the order and economy of the world.

HIS GARDEN was on the side of the mountain. I had it built mostly while he was President. It took a great deal of labor. We had to blow out the rock for the walls for the different terraces and then make the soil. ... It was a fine garden. There were vegetables of all kinds, grapes, figs, and the greatest variety of fruit. I have never seen such a place for fruit.

—EDMUND BACON

I *find friendship to be like wine, raw when new, ripened with age, the true old man's milk and restorative cordial.*

AFTER MR. JEFFERSON RETURNED from Washington, he was for years crowded with visitors, and they almost ate him out of house and home. ...We had thirty-six stalls for horses, and only used about ten of them for the stock we kept there. Very often all of the rest were full, and I had to send horses off to another place. I have often sent a wagonload of hay up to the stable, and the next morning there would not be enough left to make a hen's nest. ...He knew that it more than used up all his income from the plantation and everything else, but he was so kind and polite that he received all his visitors with a smile and made them welcome.

— EDMUND BACON

DINNER TO DARK

THE DINNER WAS ALWAYS CHOICE, and served in the French style; but no wine was set on the table till the cloth was removed. The ladies sat until about six, then retired, but returned with the tea-tray a little before seven, and spent the evening with the gentlemen; which was always pleasant, for they are obviously accustomed to join in the conversation. . . .

—GEORGE TICKNOR

SOMETIMES NATURAL PHILOSOPHY, at others politics or the arts were the topics of our conversation, for no object had escaped Mr. Jefferson; and it seemed as if from his youth he had placed his mind, as he had done his house, on an elevated situation, from which he might contemplate the universe.

—MARQUIS DE CHASTELLUX

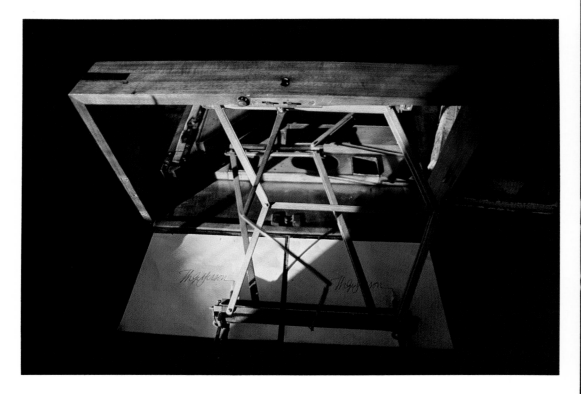

Nothing is ours, which another may deprive us of. Hence the inestimable value of intellectual pleasures. Ever in our power, always leading us to something new, never cloying, we ride serene and sublime above the concerns of this mortal world, contemplating truth and nature, matter and motion, the laws which bind up their existence, and that Eternal Being who made and bound them up by those laws.

…WHEN IT GREW TOO DARK TO READ, in the half hour which passed before candles came in, as we all sat round the fire, he taught us several childish games, and would play them with us. I remember that "Cross-questions," and "I love my Love with an A," were two I learned from him; and we would teach some of ours to him. When the candles were brought,

all was quiet immediately, for he took up his book to read; and we would not speak out of a whisper, lest we should disturb him, and generally we followed his example and took a book; and I have seen him raise his eyes from his own book, and look round on the little circle of readers and smile, and make some remark to mamma about it.

—VIRGINIA JEFFERSON TRIST

*I*f the lady has anything difficult in her disposition, avoid what is rough, and attach her good qualities to you. Consider what are otherwise as a bad stop in your harpsichord, and do not touch on it, but make yourself happy with the good ones. ... All we can do is to make the best of our friends, love and cherish what is good in them, and keep out of the way of what is bad; but no more think of rejecting them for it, than of throwing away a piece of music for a flat passage or two.

The term is not very distant, at which we are to deposit in the same cerement, our sorrows and suffering bodies, and to ascend in essence to an ecstatic meeting with the friends we have loved and lost, and whom we shall still love and never lose again.

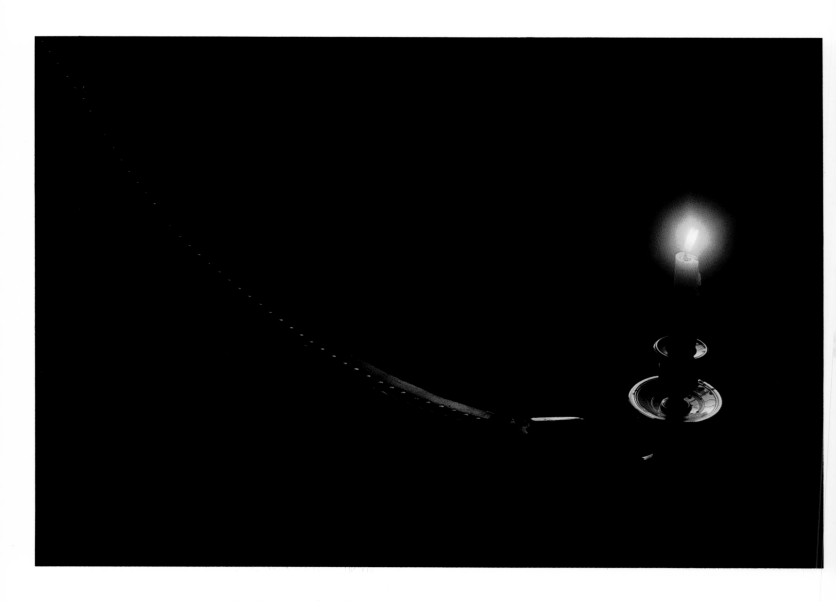

*M*an is fed with fables through life, leaves it in the belief he knows something of what has been passing, when in truth he has known nothing but what has passed under his own eye.

Floor plan of Monticello today.

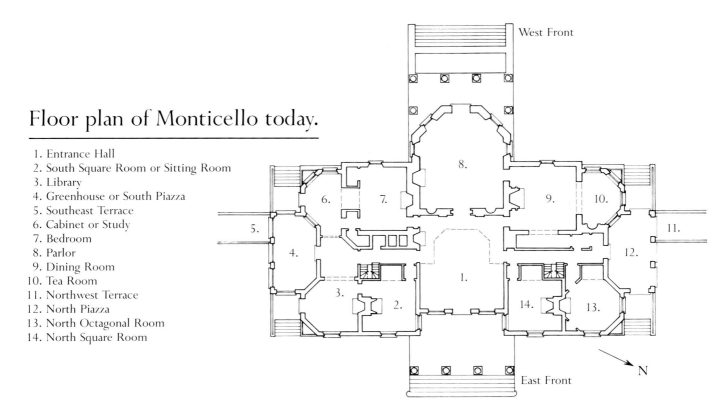

1. Entrance Hall
2. South Square Room or Sitting Room
3. Library
4. Greenhouse or South Piazza
5. Southeast Terrace
6. Cabinet or Study
7. Bedroom
8. Parlor
9. Dining Room
10. Tea Room
11. Northwest Terrace
12. North Piazza
13. North Octagonal Room
14. North Square Room

West Front

East Front

N

COMMENTARY
by Charles Granquist

2-3 MONTICELLO, WEST FRONT. Thomas Jefferson began building Monticello in 1769, when he was 26 years old. With his constant "putting up and pulling down," construction continued for the next 40 years. His original design, never completed, was extensively modified upon his return from France in 1789, and the present house, begun in 1796, was not finished until 1809, at the time of his retirement from the Presidency.

4-5 CABINET. Jefferson's Bedroom, Cabinet, and Library comprised his sanctum sanctorum. In his Cabinet, or study, he wrote the bulk of his voluminous correspondence while seated in a curious reading and writing arrangement that permitted him to work in the half-recumbent position necessitated by his rheumatic back. Surrounded by his books, papers, and scientific instruments, Jefferson could work without interruption from his family and visitors, no small luxury in so busy a household.

6 CLOCK BELL CUPOLA AND WIND VANE ON EAST PEDIMENT. Jefferson's "Meteorological Journal," compiled at Monticello between 1810 and 1816, illustrates the remarkable degree of objectivity, analysis, and perseverance that he brought to all his scientific endeavors. His observations of temperature, wind direction, precipitation, and clouds provided Jefferson and his friends with a wealth of information that could be used in making schedules for planting and in determining the varieties of plants best suited for Virginia. He noted that it might even be possible for "physicians to observe the coincidences of the diseases of each season, with the particular winds prevalent, the quantities of heat and rain, etc."

8 ENTRANCE HALL AND BUST OF JEFFERSON AFTER HOUDON. Jefferson the naturalist rebelled at the European belief —as expressed by the Comte de Buffon—that animals in America were generally smaller, fewer in species, and if of Old World stock, degenerate compared to their ancestors. The antlers, tusks, and heads of many of America's largest mammals, displayed in the Entrance Hall, refuted Buffon's claims, as Jefferson had done earlier in his *Notes on the State of Virginia.*

11 MONTICELLO TO THE SOUTHEAST.

12-13 RIVANNA RIVER. Jefferson never tired of extolling the beauty of his native Virginia and particularly his own Monticello. He wrote to Angelica Church in 1788, "I remember you told me when we parted, you would come to see me at Monticello. I have been planning what I would show you: a flower here, a tree there; yonder a grove, near it a fountain; on this side a hill, on that a river. Indeed, madam, I know nothing so charming as our own country."

14-15 MONTICELLO FROM CARTER'S MOUNTAIN. The constant construction at Monticello made it difficult for many visitors to appreciate the architecture of the house, but the beauty of the site escaped few.

Margaret Bayard Smith recalled her journey up the mountain in 1809, noting that "no vestige of the labour of man appeared; [and] nature seemed to hold undisturbed dominion." On her arrival at the house, she found "the whole surrounding scene, is eminently fitted to raise an interest beyond that which such objects ordinarily excited in the mind. Every thing, moral and physical, conspires to excite and sustain this sentiment. You stand on the summit of a mountain, on the east affording a view of an open country, presenting a most extensive and variegated prospect; on the west, north, and south, by the Allegany itself, which rising from beyond the south mountain, rears its majestic head in awful grandeur. Here, in this wild and sequestered retirement, the eye dwells with delight on the triumph of art over nature, rendered the more impressive by the unreclaimed condition of all around."

16 NECK STOCK AND SHIRT LABELED BY JEFFERSON. To his slave Isaac, Jefferson appears to have dressed fashionably. He said, "Old Master wore Vaginny cloth and a red waistcoat (all the gentlemen wore red waistcoats in dem days) and small clothes; arter dat he used to wear red breeches too."

More critical observers had different views regarding his attire. His granddaughter Ellen Wayles Coolidge recalled: "His dress was simple, and adapted to his ideas of neatness and comfort. He paid little attention to fashion, wearing whatever he liked best, and sometimes blending the fashions of several periods. He wore long waistcoats when the mode was for very short, white cambric stocks fastened behind with a buckle, when cravats were universal."

17 JEFFERSON'S BEDROOM WINDOW.

18 WEST PEDIMENT AND DOME. Whatever plans Jefferson may have had for the Dome, or "Sky Room" at Monticello, it is clear that it played no major role in the day-to-day life of the family. Margaret Bayard Smith recalled: "He afterwards took us to the drawing room, 26 or 7 feet diameter, in the dome. It is a noble and beautiful apartment, with 8 circular windows and a sky-light. It was not furnished and being in the attic story is not used, which I thought a great pity, as it might be made the most beautiful room in the house."

19 SOUTHEAST DOME ROOM WINDOW AND BUST OF JEFFERSON BY SIDNEY MORSE.

20 SITTING ROOM CURTAIN. With his usual attention to detail, Jefferson oversaw virtually every aspect of the furnishing of his house, from the purchase or production of all the "standing furniture" to the color of the walls and the designs for the curtains. His notes and memorandum books abound with descriptions and measurements of furnishings that he had seen on his travels and which he thought would suit Monticello.

21 ARGAND LAMP ON THE DINING ROOM MANTEL. No one was more pleased than Jefferson by the remarkable strides made in the improvement of lighting during the late 18th century. The Argand, or cylinder lamp as he called it, was of particular interest. He wrote Charles Thomson from Paris in 1784: "There has been a lamp called the Cylinder lamp, lately invented here. It gives a light equal as is thought to that of six or eight candles. It requires olive oil, but its consumption is not great. The improvement is produced by forming the wick into a hollow cylinder so that there is a passage for the air through the hollow."

22 JEFFERSON'S BOOTS AND WALKING STICK. Jefferson had a deep appreciation for the harmony of body and mind. He wrote to his daughter Martha in 1787, "exercise and application produce order in our affairs, health of body, cheerfulness of mind, and these make us precious to our friends."

23 LIBRARY AND CABINET.

24 WEST FRONT ENTRANCE.

25 SPECTACLES MADE TO JEFFERSON'S DESIGN.

26-27 WEST FRONT. The nine second- and third-floor chambers at Monticello were occupied by family members. The second-floor bedrooms were heated by stoves, but the entire third floor was unheated. The complex shape of the roof provided many attic cubbyholes in which the grandchildren often played hide-and-seek.

28 PARLOR TO THE SOUTHWEST. In this room were held the myriad social functions of a large and active family as well as more intimate celebrations such as marriages and christenings. Although Jefferson placed many of his finest furnishings and the bulk of his extensive art collection in the Parlor, he refused to sacrifice comfort to fashion. Flanking the door to the West Lawn, he kept a pair of Campeachy chairs, including a relatively crude version made by his slave Johnny Hemings. One of these was recalled by his granddaughter Ellen Wayles Coolidge: "In the large Parlour with its parqueted floor stood the campeachy chair, made of goatskin, and sent to him from New Orleans, where, in the shady twilight, I was wont to see him resting."

29 ENTRANCE HALL TO THE EAST. Ellen Wayles Coolidge wrote to Jefferson in 1808, "[I] went over to Monticello; I think the hall, with its gravel colored border is the most beautiful room I ever was in, without excepting the drawing rooms at Washington." Her approbation was not entirely shared by others who viewed the room, however. Benjamin P. Richardson noted in 1824 that the room reminded him "of the adornments of Romeo's apothecary shop where 'a tortoise hung, an alligator stuffed, and other skins of ill shaped fishes.'"

Presumably Ellen was more familiar with her grandfather's collecting habits than was Richardson and was prepared for the vast array of Indian artifacts, natural history specimens, antlers, and art works that confronted visitors entering Jefferson's Entrance Hall "museum." On the walls opposite and flanking his seven-day calendar clock were displayed items brought back from the Lewis and Clark expedition; the fruits of William Clark's dig for fossils at Big Bone Lick, Kentucky; as well as Jefferson's extensive collection of American Indian artifacts.

30-31 TEA ROOM TO THE SOUTH. Although the Dining Room and Tea Room were the scene of occasional formal dinners, there too were held the daily meals attended by family and guests. At meals, as in most respects, favorite guests were treated as extensions of the family, leading to scenes such as that recalled by Ellen Wayles Harrison, Jefferson's great-granddaughter.

Mrs. James Madison, an annual visitor, was seated next to Jefferson's grandson, Benjamin Franklin Randolph, and found him "unequal to the management of his muffin." When Mrs. Madison's aid was invoked, "she took the knife to cut it, but a little hand was laid on hers, and an earnest voice exclaimed 'No! No! That is not the way!' 'Well how then, Master Ben?' 'Why, you must tear him open, and put butter inside and stick holes in his back! And then pat him and squeeze him and the juice will run out!' Mrs. Madison, much amused, followed his directions."

32 DINING ROOM AND TEA ROOM. Situated on the northwest corner of the house, the Dining Room and Tea Room bear the brunt of prevailing winter winds. To reduce their effect, Jefferson installed a storm window on the triple sash window and double sliding doors in the arch leading to the Tea Room.

As in all the principal rooms, Jefferson made provisions for reading. In the Dining Room he kept a candlestand and chair near the fireplace and a selection of books on the mantel. He once observed that with a family as large as his he accomplished much of his reading while waiting for everyone to assemble for dinner.

33 COFFEE URN IN TEA ROOM. This silver coffee urn was purchased by Jefferson in Paris in 1789. It was made by Jacques Louis Auguste Leguay, and may have served as the prototype for an urn designed by Jefferson, and made by Jean Baptiste Claude Odiot, for presentation to Charles Louis Clerisseau, who had assisted Jefferson in the designs for the Virginia State Capitol building.

34-35 TEA ROOM TO THE NORTH. Owing to the size of Jefferson's family, and the number of guests, each of the public rooms at Monticello served several functions. In addition to meals and family teas, the Tea Room was the site of one of Jefferson's reading and writing arrangements, permitting him to take advantage of the late afternoon light found at the northwest corner of the house. Beneath the niche, which originally contained a small, urn-shaped stove, Jefferson often sat in an old revolving Windsor chair with writing arm, or reclined with the aid of a sofa pulled up to the chair, as was the case in his Cabinet.

36 PEDIMENTS, WEST FRONT.

37 PARLOR TO THE NORTHWEST. In 1802, Jefferson received from Philadelphia six sofas decorated with gold leaf, almost certainly in the then popular French fashion. These sofas provide a sidelight on a possible use for the Parlor. Thomas Claxton, who had helped purchase many of the furnishings for the President's House, wrote to Jefferson in 1801 regarding the sofas for Monticello: "If each one has a cushion, it will be a handsome piece of furniture in a room, but when two are placed together for purposes of sleeping on, one cushion covering both, would perhaps be more convenient."

It is easy to dismiss the notion of guests sleeping on the sofas in the Parlor as a backwoods Virginia phenomenon, but it must be remembered that Claxton was speaking from the perspective of Philadelphia's fashionable circles. In spite of potential discomfort, Jefferson ordered one cushion per sofa.

38-39 PARLOR TO THE SOUTHEAST. Visitors to Monticello

were often struck by the sometimes eccentric nature of the house and its occupants. Sir Augustus John Foster recalled his first meeting with Jefferson's grandson, Thomas Jefferson Randolph: "he was a fine young lad, and, according to what I was told was a general Custom in Virginia among Boys, he walked into the Drawing Room, without Shoes or Stockings, though very neatly dressed in other Respects. I had however, Reason to doubt afterwards that the Practice was so general and I believe it was a mere whim of his Grandfather who in the very first Conversation I had with him expressed his wonder that feet were not as often washed as hands and would I dare say, if he could have ventured it without ridicule, have been for a still greater degree of Nakedness, so fond was he of leaving Nature as unconfined as possible in all her Works."

40 SOUTH SQUARE ROOM OR SITTING ROOM. The Sitting Room, adjacent to the Library, may have served as part of Jefferson's sanctum sanctorum, but more likely it offered a retreat for the family from the other, more public, first-floor rooms. Here Jefferson installed one of five projecting fireplaces based on Count Rumford's designs for efficient heating. The radiant heat from the projection and the design of the opening and flue may have provided some slight improvement over the dismal heating abilities of the average fireplace.

41 PORTRAIT OF NICHOLAS P. TRIST AFTER NEAGLE. Nicholas P. Trist, a long-time friend of Jefferson and his family, married Jefferson's granddaughter, Virginia Jefferson Randolph, at Monticello on September 11, 1824. The young man was Jefferson's part-time secretary and constant companion until Jefferson's death in 1826.

43 LIBRARY. Jefferson once commented that he could not live without books. His Library at Monticello, which housed the bulk of his collection of some 6,000 volumes, represented the fruits of over 50 years of collecting both in America and abroad. The contents of the Library, arranged according to Sir Francis Bacon's divisions of knowledge, were as varied as its owner's interests, containing, as Jefferson noted, "what is chiefly valuable in science and literature generally, [and] extends more particularly to whatever belongs to the American statesman."

44-45 GREENHOUSE OR SOUTH PIAZZA. The South Piazza, adjacent to Jefferson's Library, served as both greenhouse and workshop. He owned an extensive assortment of tools, and as Isaac recalled, "My old Master was neat a hand as ever you see to make keys and locks and small chains, iron and brass."

As a greenhouse, the South Piazza was not particularly successful. "You enquire whether I have a hot house, greenhouse, or to what extent I pay attention to these things," Jefferson wrote to Bernard McMahon in 1811. "I have only a greenhouse, and have used that only for a very few articles. My frequent and long absences at a distant possession render my efforts even for the few greenhouse plants I aim at, abortive. During my last absence in the winter, every plant I had in it perished."

46-47 SERPENTINE WALK ON THE WEST LAWN. Considering his own enthusiasm, it would have been difficult for Jefferson's family not to have shared his love of gardening. From an early age his granddaughters eagerly followed every development in the gardens, as may be seen in the recollections of Ellen Wayles Coolidge: "…when spring returned, how eagerly we watched the first appearance of the shoots above ground. Each root was marked with its own name written on a bit of stick by its side, and what joy it was for one of us to discover the tender green breaking through the mould, and run to granpapa to announce, that we really believed Marcus Aurelius was coming up, or the Queen of the Amazons was above ground! With how much pleasure compounded of our pleasure and his own, on the new birth, he would immediately go out to verify the fact, and praise us for our diligent watchfulness…Oh, these were happy moments for us and for him!"

48 EAST FRONT. Jefferson returned from France in 1789 imbued with the latest ideas in Parisian townhouse design. He outlined these concepts, which had a profound effect on his remodeling of Monticello, in a letter to John Brown in 1797: "The method of building houses 2, 3, or 4 stories high, first adopted in cities, where ground is scarce, and thence without reason copied in the country, where ground abounds, has for these 20 or 30 years been abandoned in Europe in all good houses newly built. In Paris particularly all the new and good houses are of a single story. That is of the height of 16 or 18 feet generally, and the whole of it given to rooms of entertainment: but in the parts where there are bedrooms they have two tiers of them from 8 to 10 feet high each, with a small private staircase. By these means great staircases are avoided, which are expensive and occupy a space which would make a good room in every story."

49 MARIGOLDS AND ASTERS ON THE WEST LAWN.

50 CARRIAGE.

51 STABLES UNDER THE NORTHWEST TERRACE. As his long-time overseer Edmund Bacon noted, Jefferson was "passionately fond of a good horse." This was borne out by the prices he paid and the care he expended on each purchase. He was also a lifelong believer in the medicinal and intellectual benefits to be derived from riding. Late in life he wrote to William Short: "I can assure you from experience that to old age the daily ride is among the most cheering of comforts. It renews the pleasurable sensation that we are still in society with the beings and the things around us and so delightful and so necessary is this daily revival to me, that I would wish to lose that and life together…."

52-53 GLOBE AMARANTH.

54 LILY-FLOWERING TULIP.

55 MORNING GLORY.

56-57 PARROT TULIP. Parrot tulips were received by Jefferson as early as 1812 when Bernard McMahon shipped him "2 Roots Parrot Tulips, color of the flowers red, green and yellow mixed."

58 ONE OF A PAIR OF JEFFERSON'S BOX LOCK POCKET PISTOLS BY DEALTRY OF LONDON. To his nephew, Peter Carr, Jefferson wrote in 1785, "As to the species of exercise, I advise the gun. While this gives a moderate exercise to the body, it gives boldness, enterprise, and independence to the mind. Games played with the ball and others of that nature, are too violent for the body and stamp no character on the mind. Let your gun therefore be the constant companion of your walks."

59 GROVE AT MONTICELLO. Jefferson planned from an early date to include a Grove on the west side of the mountain, recognizing that in a southern climate, "Shade is our Elysium."

With an unswerving eye for composition, he noted in a memorandum, "The canvas at large must be Grove, of the largest trees, (poplar, oak, elm, maple, ash, hickory, chestnut, Linden, Weymouth pine, sycamore) trimmed very high, so as to give it the appearance of open ground, yet not so far apart but that they may cover the ground with close shade.

"This must be broken by clumps of thicket, as the open grounds of the English are broken by clumps of trees. Plants for thickets are broom, calycanthus, altheas, gelder rose, magnolia glauca, azalea, fringe tree, dogwood, red bud, wild crab, kalmia, mezereon, euonymus, halesia, quamoclid, rhododendron, oleander, service tree, lilac, honeysuckle, brambles."

60-61 MONTICELLO AND ROUNDABOUTS. An active plantation like Monticello required an extensive network of roads. Jefferson arranged four of the principal roads, called Roundabouts, in increasingly larger circles descending the mountain. They were connected by others, including the Farm Road, the Northern Path, and the "One in Ten" and "One in Twenty," the last two named for their grades.

The roads on the mountain were the sites of many of Jefferson's favorite rides. Not all of his guests were as taken with the sights to be found along these trails, however. Margaret Bayard Smith recalled her tour: "The first circuit, the road was good, and I enjoyed the views it afforded and the familiar and easy conversation, which our sociable gave rise to; but when we descended to the second and third circuit, fear took from me the power of listening to him, or observing the scene, nor could I forbear expressing my alarm, as we went along a rough road which had only been laid out, and on driving over fallen trees, and great rocks, which threatened an overset to our sociable and a roll down the mountains to us."

62 GROVE.

63 DOGWOOD. Dogwoods were among the plants that Jefferson watched to determine the progress of the seasons and the severity of frosts.

64 SOUTHEAST TERRACE. The Terraces covering the dependencies served as pleasant places to stroll as well as providing access to the North and South Pavilions. Jefferson also used them to augment his meager natural water supply on top of the mountain. His records indicate that the well was more often dry than full; he noted in his Garden Book in 1803, "the well was observed about a month ago to have plenty of water in it having been dry about 18 months." The rainwater runoff from the terraces, stored in four large cisterns, must have proved invaluable.

65 WEST LAWN FROM THE PARLOR.

66 NORTHWEST PRIVY ROOF AND WILLOW.

67 FISHPOND. Jefferson built several fishponds on his Albemarle properties. They were stocked primarily with carp and chub. Although the oval pond on the West Lawn near the South Pavilion was kept well stocked, its primary purpose was probably decorative.

68 OBSERVATORY IN THE CABINET. No one felt more strongly than Jefferson that "a debt of service is due from every man to his country proportional to the boundaries which nature and fortune have measured to him." Few of his peers, however, over as long a life, subordinated their own interests to those of their country as did Jefferson. "Nature intended me for the tranquil pursuits of science, by rendering them my supreme delight," he wrote Pierre Samuel du Pont de Nemours in 1809. "But the enormities of the times in which I have lived, have forced me to take a part in resisting them, and to commit myself on the boisterous ocean of political passions."

69 NASTURTIUMS. Jefferson considered nasturtiums vegetables and planted them on the Garden Terrace.

70-71 GARDEN PRODUCE.

72 CAULIFLOWER ON THE GARDEN TERRACE.

73 BEAN POLES ON THE GARDEN TERRACE. The everpresent gardener in Jefferson measured time by the arrival of crops. When away from home he was constantly reminded of, and homesick for, nature's progress at Monticello. He wrote to his daughter Maria from New York in June 1790, "We had not peas or strawberries here till the 8th day of this month. On the same day I heard the first whip-poor-will whistle. Swallows and martins appeared here on the 21st of April. When did they appear with you? and when had you peas, strawberries and whip-poor-will in Virginia? Take notice hereafter whether the whip-poor-will always come with the strawberries and peas...."

74-75 APPLE TREE. Jefferson's orchards, located on the north and south slopes of the mountain, contained an astonishing range of fruits, including nearly 150 varieties of apples, quince, cherries, peaches, apricots, plums, pears, and nectarines.

76 CITRON MELONS.

77 VEGETABLE GARDEN TERRACE. Work was begun to level the present Garden Terrace on the south slope of the mountain in 1804. The 1,000-foot length of the garden was divided into three

"platforms" with beds connected by grass walks and alleys. The first platform, Jefferson noted in 1812, contained "Fruits" such as melons, tomatoes, and beans; the second contained "Roots" such as carrots, beets, and leeks; and the third, "Leaves" such as lettuce, celery, and cauliflower.

The Terrace is supported by a stone wall that rises to a height of nearly eleven feet. Between the wall and the outermost walkway Jefferson constructed a small garden structure, 12 feet six inches square, with an arch on each side and a pyramidal roof surrounded by a Chinese railing. This pavilion was one of Jefferson's favorite retreats.

78 KITCHEN WINDOW. By locating the Kitchen beneath the corner of the Southeast Terrace, Jefferson provided all-weather access and reduced the danger to the main house in the event of fire. The prevailing winds from the northwest also tended to keep smoke and cooking odors away from the house.

79 PEPPERS.

80 WINE CELLAR. Jefferson's love of good wines was shared by many of his peers, but his interest in viticulture went far beyond that of most of his friends and acquaintances. He experimented, with little success, with grape vines at Monticello, and did not feel that in the immediate future wine production would be economically feasible in this country.

He believed strongly in the medicinal qualities of wine and cautioned that increased taxes on wine were a threat to the health of his countrymen. He observed: "No nation is drunken where wine is cheap: and none sober where the dearness of wine substitutes ardent spirits as the common beverage."

81 WINE BOTTLE. With regard to wine, as in most matters, Jefferson was a temperate man. The slave Isaac recalled that he had "never heard of his being disguised in drink," and that, in spite of having "Plenty of wine, best old Antigua rum and cider," Jefferson himself "was very fond of wine and water." Jefferson wrote to Dr. Vine Utley in 1819: "I double, however, the Doctor's glass and a half of wine, and even treble it with a friend; but halve its effects by drinking weak wines only."

82-83 KITCHEN UNDER THE SOUTHEAST TERRACE. The Kitchen at Monticello must have been a center of activity for both the household servants and the family. In spite of Jefferson's appreciation of the culinary arts, the actual preparation of food must have interested him little. His slave Isaac recalled that he "never went into the kitchen except to wind up the clock."

84 HERBS AND WILD TURKEY.

85 KITCHEN TABLE. Although Jefferson was known for the "Epicurean delicacy" of the meals served at the President's House and at Monticello, his own tastes were relatively simple. He noted to Dr. Utley in 1819, "I have lived temperately, eating little animal food, and that not as an aliment, so much as a condiment for the vegetables, which constitute my principal diet."

86-87 MONTICELLO AND DEPENDENCIES. Beneath the Terraces flanking the house to the north and south, Jefferson concealed many of the less attractive, but necessary, appurtenances of plantation life, such as the Kitchen, Smoke House, Stables, and Ice House. By building these "offices" into the hillside, he preserved the views from the Lawn. Access to the dependencies was provided by means of a passageway to the basement of the house from each corner of the Terraces.

88 DINING TABLE.

89 DINING TABLE AND DUMBWAITER. Among the many innovations that Jefferson brought back from France was the use of dumbwaiters at the dining table. Those now at Monticello were made for Jefferson in the early 1790s, probably in Philadelphia, and almost certainly resembled the dumbwaiters used by him in the President's House. These four-tiered rectilinear tables appear to be unique in American furniture. Margaret Bayard Smith described their use in Washington: "When he had any persons dining with him, with whom he wished to enjoy a free and unrestricted flow of conversation, the number of persons at table never exceed four, and by each individual was placed a *dumb-waiter,* containing everything necessary for the progress of the dinner from beginning to end, so as to make the attendance of servants entirely unnecessary, believing as he did, that much of the domestic and even public discord was produced by the mutilated and misconstructed repetition of free conversation at dinner tables, by these mute but not inattentive listeners."

90 JEFFERSON'S BEDROOM, NORTHEAST WALL. Jefferson originally installed a large French pier mirror on this wall to reflect the light from the triple sash window opposite. Adequate illumination for reading and writing was always precious to Jefferson, and the pier mirrors placed on the interior walls of the principal rooms on the west side of the house, in conjunction with large windows and the Bedroom and Dining Room skylights, enhanced the available natural light.

91 JEFFERSON'S CABINET FROM THE BEDROOM. In principle, Jefferson's alcove bed, open on both sides, allowed him to rise on either the Cabinet or Bedroom side. In practice, however, this was not possible, for he had his workmen construct a light mahogany frame, covered with paper, which he placed on the Cabinet side of the bed to reduce drafts.

At the foot of his bed, on a wall bracket, stood a French clock of his own design, consisting of a round dial supported between two black marble obelisks.

92 JEFFERSON'S POLYGRAPH. Called by Charles Willson Peale, its promoter and co-developer, "a happy contrivance of the ingenious Mr. John I. Hawkins for multiplying copies of writing," the polygraph was considered by Jefferson to be one of the great inventions of his day. He used one constantly, both at Monticello and on his travels, and was so enamored that he lent his name, as President, for the promotion of the machine. In one of his advertisements Peale included the following letter from Jefferson: "On five months full trial of the Polygraph with two pens, I can now conscientiously declare it a most precious invention. Its superiority over the copying press is so decided that I have entirely laid that aside; I only regret it had not been invented 30 years sooner, as it would have enabled me to preserve copies of my letters during the war, which to me would have been a consoling possession."

93 JEFFERSON'S OBSERVATORY IN THE CABINET. The masonry pier, covered with marble slabs, built into the south window of the Cabinet served to hold Jefferson's "observing instruments." To assist him in his observations he also kept a celestial globe and an astronomical clock in this room. He owned two fine English telescopes by Dollond, both equipped for celestial as well as terrestrial use.

94-95 LIBRARY. Jefferson sold his books to the government in 1815 to replace those burned by the British during the War of 1812. In spite of his reduced circumstances he immediately began to assemble another collection.

96 BLUE RIDGE MOUNTAINS FROM MONTICELLO.
97 SPECTACLES AND CANDLESTICK.

98-99 WEST FRONT.

101 MUSIC STAND AND PIANO. Music, Jefferson wrote, "is the favorite passion of my soul." An accomplished violinist, he passed on his love for music to his children and grandchildren on the theory that "it furnishes a delightful recreation for the hours of respite from the cares of the day, and lasts us through life."

In 1778 Jefferson went so far as to contemplate hiring his own domestic band of musicians. Writing to his Italian friend Giovanni Fabbroni, he stated that he employed a gardener, a weaver, a cabinet maker, and a stone cutter, and expressed the hope that: "In a country where, like yours, music is cultivated and practised by every class of men I suppose there might be found persons of those trades who could perform on the French horn, clarinet or hautboy and bassoon, so that one might have a band of two French horns, two clarinets and hautboys and a bassoon, without enlarging their domest[ic] expences."

102 JEFFERSON'S BEDROOM TO THE NORTHWEST. Jefferson appears to have used this chamber, for the most part, as a dressing room. Although he kept a chair and bookcase next to the fireplace, the light in the Cabinet was better for working and the stove in that room probably supplied more heat than the Bedroom fireplace.

103 JEFFERSON'S BED ALCOVE. As originally built, Jefferson's Bedroom was an 18-foot cube. Among the many alterations and additions to the house following his stay in France, he built a new wall in front of the southeast Bedroom wall, creating the present bed alcove. He included a closet in the space above the bed, reached by a stepladder from the small closet to the right of the alcove. The oval windows provided light and ventilation to the closet.

104-105 SOUTH PAVILION. The South Pavilion was the only building completed when Jefferson moved to the mountaintop in 1770. He wrote to James Ogilvie in February 1771: "I have lately removed to the mountain from whence this is dated, and with which you are not unacquainted. I have here but one room, which, like the cobbler's, serves me for parlour for kitchen and hall. I may add, for bed chamber and study too."

It was to this building that be brought his bride, the widow Martha Wayles Skelton, in January 1772, during a severe snowstorm. The accommodations apparently did not prove entirely satisfactory, for after a relatively brief stay they moved to Martha's house, Elk Hill, in Goochland County, pending further construction at Monticello.

106 ARM OF REVOLVING CHAIR WITH CANDLE HOLDER. In the last years of his life, when he approached financial ruin and Monticello and its furnishings gradually fell into a state of disrepair, Jefferson presented a somewhat pathetic figure, greeting guests in a waistcoat and breeches many years out of date and seating them in chairs whose stuffing protruded from holes in the leather seats. Appearances then as throughout his life seemed to be of little concern to Jefferson, however. As one visitor noted a few years before Jefferson's death, though the house and its furniture were in a state of dilapidation and neglect, in this state or not, they harmonized with their sage and had as he said, "a character of unique solitary grandeur elevated above the surface of common things."

NOTES ON THE PASSAGES

1 Thomas Jefferson letter to General Thaddeus Kosciusko, Monticello, February 26, 1810. Kosciusko (1746-1817) was a Polish military officer, patriot, and statesman who served the American forces during the Revolution.

9-10 Excerpts from *Jefferson and His Time,* by Dumas Malone, Boston, 1948-1981, appear in the following order: quotation in introductory paragraph, from Vol. VI, *The Sage of Monticello,* p. xviii; paragraph 1, from Vol. I, *Jefferson the Virginian,* p. 143; paragraph 2, from Vol. III, *Jefferson and the Ordeal of Liberty,* p. 222; paragraph 3, from Vol. I, pp. 144-145; paragraph 4, from Vol. I, p. 146; paragraphs 5-6, from Vol. VI, pp. 8-9; paragraph 7, from Vol. III, p. 231; paragraph 8, from Vol. III, p. 232; paragraph 9, from Vol. VI,